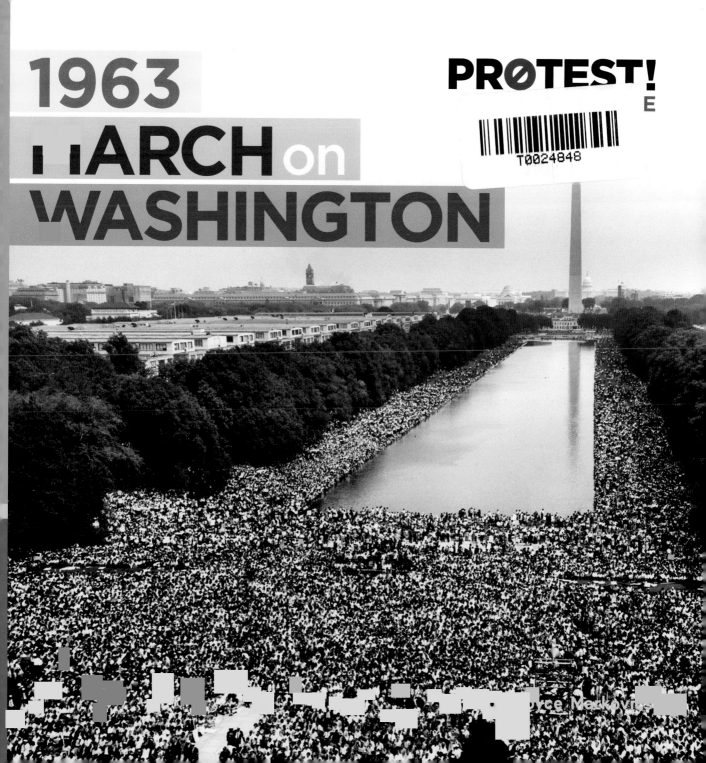

1963
MARCH on
WASHINGTON

PROTEST!

Joyce Markovics

CHERRY LAKE PRESS

Published in the United States of America by Cherry Lake Publishing Group
Ann Arbor, Michigan
www.cherrylakepublishing.com

Reading Adviser: Marla Conn, MS Ed., Literacy specialist, Read-Ability, Inc.
Content Adviser: Emilye Crosby, PhD
Book Designer: Ed Morgan

Photo Credits: Courtesy of U.S. Archives and Records Administration, cover and title page; Courtesy of Library of Congress, 4–5; Courtesy of Library of Congress, 6; Courtesy of Library of Congress, 7 top; Courtesy of Library of Congress, 7 bottom; Courtesy of U.S. Archives and Records Administration, 8; Courtesy of Library of Congress, 9; freepik.com, 9 background; © Everett Collection/Shutterstock, 10; Courtesy of Library of Congress, 11; © neftali/Shutterstock, 12; © Everett Historical/Shutterstock, 13; Wikimedia Commons, 13 top; © Katherine Welles/Shutterstock, 14 bottom; Wikimedia Commons, 15; Courtesy of Library of Congress, 16; Wikimedia Commons, 17 top; Courtesy of U.S. Archives and Records Administration, 17 bottom; Courtesy of U.S. Archives and Records Administration, 18; Courtesy of U.S. Archives and Records Administration, 19; Courtesy of U.S. Archives and Records Administration, 20; Courtesy of U.S. Archives and Records Administration, 21.

Cherry Lake Press is an imprint of Cherry Lake Publishing Group.

Library of Congress Cataloging-in-Publication Data
Names: Markovics, Joyce L., author.
Title: 1963 March on Washington / by Joyce Markovics.
Description: Ann Arbor, Michigan : Cherry Lake Publishing, [2021] | Series:
   Protest! march for change | Includes bibliographical references and
   index. | Audience: Grades 2-3
Identifiers: LCCN 2020038468 (print) | LCCN 2020038469 (ebook) | ISBN
   9781534186309 (hardcover) | ISBN 9781534186385 (paperback) | ISBN
   9781534186460 (pdf) | ISBN 9781534186545 (ebook)
Subjects: LCSH: March on Washington for Jobs and Freedom (1963 :
   Washington, D.C.)–Juvenile literature. | Civil rights
   demonstrations–Washington (D.C.)–History–20th century–Juvenile
   literature. | Civil rights movements–United States–History–20th
   century–Juvenile literature. | African Americans–Civil
   rights–History–20th century–Juvenile literature.
Classification: LCC F200 .M345 2021 (print) | LCC F200 (ebook) | DDC
   323.1196/073009046–dc23
LC record available at https://lccn.loc.gov/2020038468
LC ebook record available at https://lccn.loc.gov/2020038469

Printed in the United States of America
Corporate Graphics

CONTENTS

COMING TOGETHER

The morning of August 28, 1963, was warm and damp. Ericka Jenkins, a Black teenager, watched as a sea of people arrived in Washington, D.C. Some had traveled for days to reach her home city. "I've never been so **awestruck**," she said. "They came every way . . . buses, station wagons, cars, motorcycles, bicycles."

People from different backgrounds were pouring into Washington for an important reason. They were going to march for equal rights for Black Americans.

Jay Hardo, who was 82 years old, rode his bike from Dayton, Ohio, all the way to Washington, D.C. Another man, Ledger Smith, roller-skated 700 miles (1,127 kilometers) to get there!

By 9:00 a.m., around 40,000 people had gathered near the Washington Monument. They spread out blankets and sang songs about freedom. Ericka followed the crowds. She had never seen so many Black people in one place. And there were White people too. They were all going to march together.

Marchers cooled their feet in the Reflecting Pool near the Washington Monument.

"I saw people laughing and listening and standing very close to one another," Ericka said. "Their eyes were open, they were *listening*. I had never seen anything like that."

Gospel singer Mahalia Jackson

Famous musicians sang and played for the crowd. They included singers Mahalia Jackson, Odetta, and Bob Dylan.

The crowd continued to swell. By early afternoon, over 2,000 buses had dropped off more than 100,000 people. It was turning into the largest **protest** in U.S. history! Together, around 250,000 people—young and old, rich and poor—began to march to the Lincoln Memorial.

Thousands of people gathered at the Lincoln Memorial.

Within the Lincoln Memorial is a large statue of Abraham Lincoln. It honors the president who helped end slavery. That's where civil rights leaders, including Dr. Martin Luther King Jr., would speak and change the course of history.

Many marchers held signs or wore "March on Washington" buttons pinned to their clothing.

The protest was also known as the March on Washington for Jobs and Freedom. At the time, Black people had fewer freedoms and less access to jobs.

WHAT LED TO THE MARCH?

For hundreds of years, Black people were **enslaved** in America. Slavery ended in 1865 after the **Civil War**. But Black Americans still did not have equal rights. In the South, rules called Jim Crow laws kept them **segregated**.

A painting of enslaved people being forced to work on a large farm, or plantation

By law, Black people were not allowed to go to many of the same restaurants, hospitals, and schools as White people. Black schools often had fewer books and supplies. Also, Black people had to use separate water fountains and ride in the backs of the buses. If they broke these rules, they could be thrown in jail or even killed.

Because of **discriminatory** laws, Black families could only buy homes in certain areas. These neighborhoods were usually run-down.

Living under Jim Crow laws was terrifying for Black people. However, there were Americans who stood up against racism. Asa Philip Randolph was a Black labor leader In the 1900s. He wanted better jobs and pay for Black workers.

Asa Philip Randolph

In 1941, Randolph took on the U.S. government. He called for equal rights for Black **defense** workers. Randolph and other **activists** planned a march on Washington. When President Franklin D. Roosevelt finally agreed to help protect these workers, the march was called off. However, Randolph never forgot the idea. A big march could be a powerful tool for racial **justice**.

Black workers in the South

Another strong leader was Dr. Martin Luther King Jr. He believed that Black people deserved the same rights as White people. In 1955, King was a young **pastor** in Montgomery, Alabama, when an event on a city bus changed his life. A Black woman named Rosa Parks refused to give up her bus seat to a White man. Afterward, she was arrested.

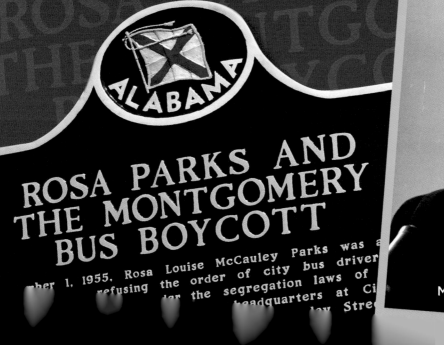

ROSA PARKS AND THE MONTGOMERY BUS BOYCOTT

...ber 1, 1955, Rosa Louise McCauley Parks was a... ...refusing the order of city bus driver... ...der the segregation laws of... ...headquarters at Ci... ...lay Stre...

Martin Luther King Jr.

E. D. Nixon, an activist who worked with Randolph, helped start the "bus boycott." King eagerly joined him. During the protest, Black people stopped riding city buses in Montgomery. The 382-day protest led to a court decision that made segregation illegal. King rose to fame as a national civil rights leader.

Nine months before Rosa Parks's arrest, 15-year-old Claudette Colvin refused to give up her seat to a White woman on a Montgomery bus. "It's my constitutional right to sit here," she bravely said to the policemen removing her from the bus.

Claudette Colvin

"I HAVE A DREAM"

In June 1963, after years of fighting for change, Randolph, King, and others planned a protest march on Washington. "Something dramatic must be done," said King. They asked Bayard Rustin, an activist and friend of Randolph's, to organize the event. He was gifted at planning. Rustin figured out all the details of the march in less than two months.

Bayard Rustin made sure marchers had everything they needed. This included food, bathrooms, and medical care!

John Lewis

Civil rights activist John Lewis was the youngest speaker. With passion and force, he said, "America, wake up! For we cannot stop, and we will not and cannot be patient."

The organizers had planned on 100,000 people attending the march. When 250,000 showed up from across the country, they were thrilled. Randolph spoke first. Others took the stage after him, delivering powerful speeches. Finally, Randolph introduced King.

King stepped up to the stage. The crowd cheered. He spoke slowly and movingly. He talked of the need for freedom, equality, and justice.

Now is the time to lift our nation from the quicksands of racial injustice to the solid rock of brotherhood. . . . I have a dream that one day . . . the sons of former slaves and the sons of former slave owners will be able to sit down together . . . I have a *dream* today!

Shouts of joy filled the mall. Randolph listened and wept. It was one of the greatest speeches—and greatest gatherings in support of Black Americans—in U.S. history.

People who couldn't attend the march watched the speeches on TV.

ACTION AND CHANGE

After years of protests and the march, the Civil Rights Act of 1964 was passed. It outlawed discrimination based on race and color. It also helped push schools to end segregation. Not long after, in 1965, the Voting Rights Act was passed. It stopped discrimination in voting.

"From every mountainside, let freedom ring!" King famously said on that warm August day. The March on Washington led to important changes, allowing freedom to ring more truly for Black Americans than it ever had. But more changes are still needed, and the march for freedom continues to this day.

The new law helped thousands more Black Americans vote.

TIMELINE

1941
June 25
Asa Philip Randolph has the idea of a march on Washington, D.C., to demand equal rights protection for Black workers.

1955
December 5
Dr. Martin Luther King Jr. leads the Montgomery bus boycott.

1963
June 20 and 21
Randolph and King announce that there will be a march in Washington, D.C.

July 2
Bayard Rustin is chosen as the head organizer of the March on Washington.

August 28
The March on Washington draws over 250,000 people; King delivers his famous "I Have a Dream" speech.

1964
July 2
Congress passes the Civil Rights Act of 1964.

1965
August 6
Congress passes the Voting Rights Act.

GLOSSARY

activists (AK-tuh-vists) people who join together to fight for a cause

awestruck (AW-struhk) filled with astonishment or respect at the sight of something

boycott (BOI-kot) the act of refusing to buy or use something as a punishment or protest

civil rights (SIV-uhl RITES) the rights everyone should have to freedom and equal treatment under the law, regardless of who they are

Civil War (SIV-uhl WOR) the war between the U.S. North and South fought over slavery and states' rights from 1861 to 1865

constitutional (kahn-stih-TOO-shuh-nuhl) relating to the laws governing a country

defense (dih-FENS) relating to the military

discriminatory (dih-SKRIM-uh-nuh-tawr-ee) characterized by unfair treatment of others based on differences in such things as skin color, age, or gender

enslaved (en-SLAYVD) kept as a slave, which is a person who is owned by another person and thought of as property

justice (JUHS-tis) the quality of being fair and good

labor (LAY-bur) relating to work

monument (MAHN-yuh-muhnt) a structure built to honor a person or event

national (NASH-uh-nuhl) relating to a country

pastor (PAS-tur) the person who's in charge of a church

protest (PROH-test) an organized public gathering to influence or change something

racism (REY-siz-uhm) a system of beliefs and policies based on the idea that one race is better than another

segregated (SEG-rih-gate-id) kept apart from another group, such as Black people separated from White people

FIND OUT MORE

Books

Evans, Shane W. *We March*. New York: Square Fish Books, 2016.

Henderson, Leah. *Together We March: 25 Protest Movements That Marched into History*. New York: Atheneum Books, 2021.

Kluger, Jeffrey. *Raise Your Voice: 12 Protests That Shaped America*. New York: Philomel Books, 2020.

Websites

Britannica Kids—March on Washington
https://kids.britannica.com/students/article/March-on-Washington/329115

NAACP—I Have a Dream: March on Washington Speech
https://www.naacp.org/i-have-a-dream-speech-full-march-on-washington

YouTube—Smithsonian: The March on Washington
https://www.youtube.com/watch?v=Qfo7rN7AIu4

INDEX

ABOUT THE AUTHOR

Joyce Markovics is a writer and history buff. She loves learning about people and telling their stories. This book is dedicated to all the people who march for a more just future.